for

ons

NFER-NELSON

The Economics of Selection

Published by The NFER-NELSON Publishing Company Ltd.,
Darville House, 2 Oxford Road East,
Windsor, Berkshire, SL4 1DF

and

242 Cherry Street, Philadelphia, PA 19106 – 1906.
Tel: (215) 238 0939. Telex: 244489

First published 1985
© 1985 David C Duncan

Library of Congress Cataloguing in Publication data

Duncan. David C.
The Economics of Selection.
Bibliography: 0.
1. Manpower Planning.   I. Title.
HF5549.5.M3D86   1985   658.3'01   85-10546
ISBN 0-7005-0672-1

ISBN 0-7005-0672-1
Code 8182 02 1

Photoset in Rockwell by Illustrated Arts Limited, Sutton, Surrey.

Contents

Author's Preface

First, a personal note. I spent my first year at the University of St. Andrews reading English, History and Latin with the long-term career aim of being a teacher, but with the immediate aim of being a fighter pilot in the RAF. This gave useful experience in surmounting selection hurdles. There were thirteen examinations to be passed with the University Air Squadron. This was followed by three days of intelligence and aptitude testing at Tor Abbey in Devon – the Aircrew Selection Battery. The next hurdle was learning to fly a Tiger Moth solo after just twelve hours tuition. We were drilled like guardsmen, but in spite of all these trials our morale remained high – we were an elite.

After all that, we were all made redundant; because after the first three years of the War, the RAF lost so few aircrews that they required no more. But they did need clerks, so we were sent to the Record Offices to do routine clerical work. There I became fascinated by problems of morale, because although discipline was comparatively lax, morale among the redundant aircrew engaged in monotonous jobs was very low, and the officers discovered that in the absence of high morale, attempts to tighten discipline failed. The only books in the camp library which dealt with the subject were Charles Oakley's *Men at Work* and Norman Maier's *Psychology in Industry*, both of which were concerned with industrial psychology.

I am much indebted to these writers, and was so impressed by their work that I decided to become an industrial psychologist. After studying philosophy, psychology and economics to degree level, I finally became an economic psychologist, since when I have been concerned to apply the hard-learned techniques of psychology in economic contexts.

The Economics of Selection is the result of some thirty years of professional experience in the selection field, and although there are no experiments in the book it reflects careful and systematic observations conducted over a long period. The approaches described are those which have been tried and found useful.

I acknowledge a considerable debt to the National Institute of Industrial Psychology, where I acquired a basic model of rational selection; also to Management Selection Limited, where I learnt to use it effectively; and to Austin Knight Limited, where I learnt many secrets of effective recruitment advertising.

Consultant Editor's Preface

It is rare for a publication to break new ground in the personnel field, but we think that this booklet does so. The costs of most operations in a business are monitored closely, particularly in modern economic conditions, but the costing of manpower decisions is, surprisingly, a neglected area. The author is well-equipped by original training and many years of experience to attempt to combine the views of an economist and an occupational psychologist.

The costing of the obvious operations of advertising and interviewing is easy, as is the costing of the interviewer's time; but the consequences of a less-than-optimum selection decision lead us into a complex, but important, area of study. David Duncan has pointed the way in this booklet, although I am sure he is not implying that he has all the answers for us! If this booklet encourages others to probe various aspects of the economics of selection in more depth it will have achieved part of its purpose, but our main hope is that managers will use it to review what they are doing in their selection and use of people. The topic seemed to have the potential to help this series of booklets to contribute in a relevant way to the practice of personnel management.

Mac Bolton
Roffey Park Management College
November 1984

Why 'The Economics of Selection'?

The title has been chosen to indicate that a rather special view of selection is being taken, concentrating not so much on the refinement of techniques as on their effectiveness in achieving their intended purpose. Lionel Robbins (1932) defined economic science as 'the science which studies human behaviour as the relationship between ends and scarce means with limited uses', and this is the definition which will be followed in this book.

Economics is not only concerned with human behaviour at the national level, for example in maximising the gross national product, or reducing unemployment; it is just as much concerned with the problems of the miner's wife trying to make do when her husband is on strike, or of the employer aiming to be efficient in his selection. The 'end' considered here will be efficient selection, and the 'scarce means', waste of which must be avoided, are time, money and human ability.

It is important not to waste time because the selection of candidates is often a competitive business, and the whole purpose of selection can be defeated if, by the time an offer is made, the candidate has had to accept another job. It is important not to waste money, both because attracting a field of applicants can be very expensive, and merits careful attention, and also because the time spent by personnel and other managers in selection is never free of charge.

Conserving human ability is also important, because although able people may be very productive in monotonous jobs, and gratifying to their employers, it may not serve their own best interests to stay in such jobs. There is a conflict of interest here between the young executive, who wants to reach the top in the shortest possible time, and his manager, who wants to maintain his outstanding performance in his present job for as long as possible.

Both time and money can be applied in a wide variety of ways, so 'limited uses' in the definition refers mainly to human ability. The important principle of equality of opportunity in employment means that we all have the right to try to be Sebastian Coe, John Ogden, John Betjeman or Francis Bacon, but does not mean that we can expect to earn a living at it. Nor does it mean that anyone has the ability to do any job, and efficient selection must begin by recognising the essential limitations of human ability and the minimum standards of ability required in a job, so that difficulties in learning or carrying it out are minimised. Equality of opportunity also brings with it a much greater choice of possible jobs for the individual, so that personal distastes, and an individual's dis-like of a job which he is able to do, will become much more important as deciding factors. For example, a graduate who has spent years studying a particular subject may well find distasteful the notion that the best course of action, in order to secure immediate well-paid employment, is to abandon the favourite subject and allow an employer to utilise the trained analytical abilities developed at university within an entirely different field.

Costing for Manpower Decisions

The sub-title of this book is 'Costing for Manpower Decisions'. To the economist, it comes naturally to apply the measuring stick of money to human behaviour, if only because he regards other ways of measuring human effort as a very difficult business. The psychologist is more often concerned to emphasise the limitations of monetary measurement, particularly where human effort is concerned, and to stress the unquestionable importance of the non-financial factors involved in work. The manager in industry concerned with manpower decisions is likely to know that selection is not merely a matter of paying more money to attract employees from a major competitor. The personnel manager may well know exactly where ninety per cent of his budget was wasted, but only after the event.

This booklet will not be concerned with costs alone, but with successful selection carried out in the most economical way, and with the means of improving the prediction of outcomes. A recent review by Monahan and Muchinsky (1983) of thirty years of personnel selection research made no mention of the economic aspects of selection, so that it seems that the subject has been neglected for too long. The ideas which follow may help to direct attention to the improvement of procedures and their evaluation.

The Economics of Manpower Planning

Looking ahead 'To the blind, all things are sudden' says a Chinese proverb; and some of the most disastrous appointments are those which have been made in a hurry, by employers who had no clear idea either of the important aspects of the job to be performed, or of the sort of person they were looking for; merely an impression of the pressing need to 'find a successor to Bloggs'.

The lack of planning arises partly because employees are not recognised as a significant part of the capital of a firm, which is the subject of monetary investment and which is carefully accumulated. Rather they are regarded as consumables, there to be exploited; or perishables, an unwise choice for long-term investment. This in turn originates from the British definition of capital.

Alfred Marshall, the British economist, defined capital as 'that which can be sold' and our banks and investors, when deciding whether to invest in a business, tend to take a pessimistic view and ask themselves 'what is the break-up value of this enterprise?', which effectively excludes people, since they are not owned by the business.

It is interesting, however, that where there is a tradition of transfer fees, as in soccer in Britain, a struggling club can maintain its finances by spotting and training youthful talent, to be transferred at a price, in due course, to the more prosperous clubs. It is a characteristic of human skills that they take time to develop, so that supply does not grow quickly, but demand for them can increase suddenly, and die off almost as suddenly. The result is that extra demand can greatly increase monetary rewards, but dying demand means an oversupply of skilled people.

Investment in Human Capital The classic American definition of capital was provided by Irving Fisher (1906). He defined capital as 'that which generates income'. This has the advantage that it includes human capital, and recognises that good employees are a good investment, as they can significantly contribute to the income of a company. This is particularly true of the post-industrial society, where more and more of the monotonous jobs are done electronically, and humans can concentrate on the more interesting and demanding occupations.

Computers and robots, however, are quite as much at risk from technological change as human beings. In the face of change, which seems to come faster every year, the inflexibility of machines becomes an investor's trap: no sooner have I bought my computer than it is obsolete. But humans can always be retrained and taught to cope with change. There are two aspects of looking ahead in costing selection: one short-term and one long-term.

Short-term Aspects

In the short term there is a variety of costs of recruitment, many of which are borne before anyone at all is selected: recruitment advertising, bringing candidates for interview, and the administrative costs of selection. When a candidate is selected, the cost of his pay, insurance and fringe benefits immediately starts to mount. It is unusual for new employees to be instantly as productive as experienced ones, and it may be necessary to bear the cost, not only of investment in training, but also of gaining experience.

Thus, in managerial economics, there is a concept of a 'break-even' point which is the time at which an employee, by playing an effective part in increasing the turnover or profits of a company, recoups the company's investment in his or her recruitment, selection and training. An experienced and able employee who needs minimum training will reach the break-even point soonest. Part of the rationale of recruiting graduates is that whatever the training, they will absorb it more quickly, accept responsibility sooner and so reach break-even point earlier. A similar philosophy underlines the use of intelligence and aptitude tests to secure employees who will adapt easily, learn quickly and perform well at an early stage.

On the other hand, employers need to be alert to spot signs of risk or instability in employees, as there is always the possibility that they will leave before the break-even point is reached so that the employer's investment in recruitment, selection and training is largely wasted. The stability of an employee assumes a special importance where the period of training is a long one, or where the skill is especially scarce. Scarce skills give rise to excessive expenditure on recruitment advertising, as employers urgently compete to fill important vacancies. Because of the shortage, the price of the skill rises, and the quality of candidate available at a given salary declines. Unstable or poor quality candidates can make good progress by making each employer a stepping stone to the next. In this situation, the prospects of reaching the break-even point with any consistency recedes. In new fields where up-to-date knowledge is at a premium, for example in the electronics industry, this consideration occasionally results in the 'hoarding' of executives.

Break-even is a backward-looking concept related to the recovery of historical costs, and the cost of instability is the cost of replacing the person who is leaving.

Long-term Aspects   Beyond the break-even point there is a forward-looking budgetary concept which considers the individual in terms of 'pay-off', which is the contribution they make to turnover and profit, less the cost of employing them. Broadly speaking, the pay-off is at its highest when the employee has sufficiently benefited from training to be maximally productive. The current market value of the employee cannot be ignored in this calculation. On occasions the experience and training gained by a manager may so increase his market value that he must be promoted, up-graded, or paid for increased responsibility.

In business it is readily recognised that capital machinery depreciates with use, and it is accordingly written down in value annually until it is finally written off. Humans, on the other hand, have a much longer productive life than most capital machinery. Their pay-off in the long term does tend to decline, in that their contribution remains constant while their salary increases. Long-service employees are considered then not so much in terms of pay-off contribution as in terms of replacement costs. These, of course, include not only recruitment and selection costs, but also the costs of mistakes which the newcomer might make.

For any job at a particular point of time, there is an upper salary limit beyond which the job-holder is not worth what he or she is paid. In the negative sense, the costs of keeping a manager in a specific job gradually increase, and there may come a point where the pay-off to employing a manager is so little that the manager has to be advised that the upper limit of salary has been reached. Then the individual may accept the situation, or seek early retirement or redundancy, or seek another job. There are disadvantages to this in that competitors without know-how can secure a disproportionate pay-off by recruiting an experienced man with technical competence.

Although academic psychologists appear to have ignored the evaluation of human capital in their writings, some attention has been given to this in America by a number of psychologists and economists in theoretical and model-making work, stemming originally from the work of H. A. Simon (1957). Arising from this is the work of Cyert and March (1963) formulating a behavioural theory of the firm. This study is pitched at the level of the firm and its decision-making processes, rather than at the individual level with which we are concerned, but they recognise the hoarding or empire-building behaviour which we mentioned, as 'organisational slack'. The economist Williamson (1963) in formulating a 'managerial' theory of the firm refers to it as 'management slack'. American economists Becker (1964) and Schultz (1961), in considering the evaluation of national programmes of education and training (including health and safety), have further developed the concept of human capital as a long-term national investment. The short-term historical cost aspects of investment in human capital have been given some attention by the psychologist Likert (1967), and the Barry Corporation scheme which he initiated has been described by Brummet et al. (1969).

In the United Kingdom, the Institute of Cost and Management Accountants cooperated with the Institute of Personnel Management in an investigation into 'human asset accounting' which was reported on by Giles and Robinson (1972). This suggested the price earnings ratio as a useful tool for determining human asset values, and did take account of human assets in the long term. Cannon (1979) however, in considering cost-effectiveness in relation to personnel decisions, expressed doubts as to whether measures of human assets added much to the stock of knowledge for decision-making purposes. He may be right for short-term, crisis decisions; in the long term, managers ignore the value of human capital at their peril, and its importance will increase in the future rather than diminish. Bridge (1981) has a more comprehensive account of the measurement of human capital than is possible here.

Management: Grow or Buy?

There are considerable arguments in favour of a company's growing its own management. As will be shown in later parts of this book, the cost of recruiting a manager from outside can be as much as thirty per cent of his annual salary. The salary paid for a particular post is also likely to be considerably inflated by the cost of tempting someone out of a similar job elsewhere. To persuade an executive to leave a post where his competence and standing are in no doubt, and to move home and family, is liable to require an increase of some twenty per cent in salary, and there is no absolute guarantee that he or she will be either competent or well thought of in the new post.

Long-service managers are least likely to leave; not only do they have little experience of the problems of changing jobs so that they fail to present themselves in the best light in letters of application and in interviews, but they can also incur considerable losses in pension rights, and are more conscious of the insecurity of changing jobs. On the other hand, there are some arguments in favour of buying managers from the market. The most common reason is expansion: a firm which is expanding fast will quickly run out of managers to promote. Another reason is diversification, where the expansion takes the company into new fields, of which its existing managers have no experience. A third is cross-fertilisation, where the company depends on managers recruited from outside to introduce new techniques, new procedures, and new ways of looking at problems.

There are, however, associated risks to be carried, and one of the benefits of long experience is the capacity to avoid expensive mistakes. The vigour and enthusiasm of new employees are valuable in the reward-seeking behaviour, which increases turnover and profits, but it carries risks if they are ignorant of the threats to avoid. This can happen even at senior levels. The new Managing Director of a major consumer goods company was so impressed by the savings made by Marks & Spencer in eliminating paperwork that he instituted a paperwork purge. Unfortunately, he did not sufficiently specify the limits to this and the sales force spent the next three months asking customers how much they owed the company for goods actually delivered, as the records had been destroyed in the drive for economy.

The Importance of Personnel Specification in Manpower Planning

Some underlying policy considerations in manpower planning have been considered. How are they translated into practice? The first step for any employer is to have a clear idea of what he is looking for. Not only will it protect him from selecting failures, and improve his chances of finding and selecting successful candidates, it will also provide candidates with a clear picture of what is expected of them. The personnel specification process embodies three themes which are central to the economics of selection: **threat avoidance, success seeking**, and **optimisation.**

Threat avoidance implies that the employer should take care to benefit from any previous unfortunate experience with candidates. The most spectacular of these come under the heading of 'critical incidents': incidents of low probability, so that they are difficult to embody in a formal job specification, but which constitute dangers to be avoided at all costs as they can be a direct cause of employment being terminated. Fiddling expense accounts or embezzling the petty cash are typical examples.

Difficulties and distastes are more routine matters for consideration. Were there any aspects of the job which were so distasteful to the present holder as to alienate him, and deprive him of satisfaction from it? What special difficulties did the job present to previous holders? Consideration of these may suggest a redesign of the job to make it easier or more palatable; more usually their implication will be a search for a candidate to whom the distastes will not matter, and who will see the difficulties as challenges.

Threat avoidance also necessitates a definition of the minimum standards permissible in a job. Is it necessary to be able to read or calculate and if so, at what speed? Is the employer willing to train his secretaries to type; and if not, what minimum standard is required? In these, the minimum demands of the job are considered and translated into requirements in the way of minimum experience, qualifications and the personality of the candidate to be appointed.

There are two ways in which these are translated into action. One is by identification in the candidate of a stigma, or some undesirable characteristic which makes his appointment completely impossible, however desirable any of his other qualities. More general is the concept of a threshold in certain characteristics above which every candidate must perform in order to be acceptable.

Success seeking is the optimistic side of the specification, and defines the positive pay-off which investment in a good candidate can bring. This is not only a matter of maintaining essential services or production, or of ensuring the continuance of duties which have been carried out in the past. Each new appointment carries with it the possibility of further expansion of business, reaching new targets of turnover or profit, or providing new services which have not been provided before. This implies a search for a better person than the previous incumbent, someone who will bring more ability, more energy, and more up-to-date knowledge than his predecessor. It also implies a specification in terms of the ideal person and the most desirable characteristics.

Optimisation brings in a reality principle. It is one thing to specify an ideal candidate, quite another thing to find one at the necessary salary level. At one extreme, there may be knowledge and experience demanded which is so rare that acceptance thresholds in other respects may be lowered, and even a stigma might be overlooked. More usually there are enough candidates for minimum thresholds of ability and personality to be met, and a compensatory process is applied, with the more desirable features of each candidate being traded off against the less desirable.

In drawing up a specification the more systematic employers will decide to which characteristics they will attach most weight in selection. A thoroughgoing approach to selection produces a lexicographic model. In this, each desirable characteristic is given a numerical weighting; each candidate is given a numerical rating for each characteristic; and weight and rating are multiplied to give a factor score. Adding the factor scores gives a final score for each candidate. This approach has its value in that it cannot be carried out by someone ignorant of the demands of the job to be filled, and it compels attention to a comprehensive assessment of the candidate against a defined specification.

The optimising approach does not regard a job description as unchangeable. Particularly at senior levels, once a candidate is chosen, the job itself will be altered to take advantage of his strengths, and so that any weaknesses in his knowledge and experience are supported by drawing on the expertise of others. However, the benefits from carrying out a thorough analysis of the job to be done, leading to a carefully compiled specification of the person, will be realised when optimising is found to be the fine tuning on the clear tone of the defined characteristics.

The Economics of Recruitment Advertising

Perhaps the greatest economies which can be made in the total selection procedure lie in the field of recruitment advertising, which can be very cost-effective if continuously evaluated, and very expensive if ignored. The author has carefully studied the many influences making for effective recruitment advertising and the advice here is based on his personal conclusions.

The considerations to be borne in mind are well illustrated by the practical example given below of an advertisement for a Finance Director. The media and their costs will be given later. The example is fictitious, but it has been made as realistic as possible.

FINANCE DIRECTOR   **South London**
Retail Multiple   **£20,000 plus**
Our client is an expanding and profitable chain of 20 stores averaging 20,000 sq.ft., spread throughout the Home Counties. The Finance Director will be responsible to the Board for staffing, programming and controlling some 75 geographically dispersed costing and accounting staff, and for ensuring that accurate computerised results of daily trading are promptly available.

Candidates should be at least 30, with professional accounting qualifications and responsible experience in the financial control of retail operations. Salary at least £20,000 p.a. plus car. Non-contributory pension. Removal expenses paid. Please send CV to D. C. Duncan at 21 Princes Street, London W1R 7RG.

RECRUITMENT ADVERTISEMENT

Length of Advertisement Apart from the heading, the main body of this advertisement comprises some 600 characters. Allowing six characters per word this is 100 words. Systematic research has shown that in the most expensive media there are diminishing returns from a size greater than a five-inch double column. (The modern equivalent is 13 cm. double, i.e. twenty-six single column centimetres.) The text has been tailored to fit within this size restriction.

Title of Advertisement For an advertisement to be read it must first attract attention. Display advertisements justify their costs in attracting a greater response from relevant candidates. This permits a prominent title, and all researchers agree that a bold title is of vital importance. In the author's experience the title should occupy up to twenty-five per cent of the available space. In the example, the title gives the salary, the location, the type of business, and what the job is about. The title does not necessarily give the name by which the holder is known once in office, since this may convey the wrong impression. If the post in the example was advertised as 'Department Head – Administration' the response would undoubtedly suffer. If salary is omitted, candidates assume it is modest. If location is omitted, candidates may withdraw on discovering that it is in a part of the country where they would prefer not to work. Mention of the sector of industry increases the relevance of candidates.

An interesting grammatical point is that to gain impact with economy of words, noun-adjectives, so detested by linguistic purists, are regularly used in titles. 'Engineer to Work with Concrete' becomes 'Concrete Engineer', and 'Director of Finance' becomes 'Finance Director' in our example. Effective advertising is not always good grammar!

Content of Advertisement
Restrictions imposed by the size of the advertisement and the prominence given to the title necessitate economy in the use of words. As long as the text is legible it can be set in small type, because once the attention of applicants has been drawn to the advertisement, they will read the text. A more important consideration, perhaps, is that one extra word may add at least £40 to the total cost of an advertisement. So each word is examined to ensure that it justifies its inclusion, and each part of the advertisement is composed to maximise its effectiveness.

The first sentence is designed to 'flow', with adjectives describing the employer in favourable terms and mentioning achievements of which he is proud, as well as conveying encouraging and accurate information. The second sentence also 'flows', using verbs to describe what the Finance Director will do, to whom and for whom he will be responsible and for what. Up to this point, the advertisement is trying to attract interest, arouse desire and secure a maximum response. The third sentence is designed to limit the field to the most relevant candidates by stipulating age range, qualifications and experience required. The advertisement given in the example is relatively lenient, as accountants are not gamblers by nature, and only apply for jobs which they feel are just right for them. Salesmen, whose criterion is whether they would like the job, require much tighter advertising. The final part of the advertisement mentions the rewards and conditions for the appointment, and specifies what action should be taken. Economy of words is vital at this stage. There is nothing to be gained by 'flow': 'cable language' is quite adequate, and the danger of wasted words is great.

Candidates hate box numbers at the end of the advertisement, but like names. A telephone number will secure a speedy response. Response analysis is made possible by using a different letter code for each medium used. The Appendix 'Checklist for Advertisements' provides a more detailed guide to the desirable content.

What motivates candidates to reply to advertisements written this way? Expressed in terms of the motivator model of Frederick Herzberg (1966), a recruitment advertisement is an appeal to the **motivators.** According to Herzberg, the bad news about work, which he calls **hygiene factors**, are quite different in kind from the good news, which he calls motivators. Recruitment advertising embodies the good news about work, and accentuates the positive aspects of any job, such as the prospect of increased salary, promotion, responsibility, variety and challenge. In candidate interviews, the hygiene factors, such as inconsiderate bosses or workmates, poor working conditions, low pay and insecurity, emerge as reasons for wishing to change jobs, but the candidate usually assumes that the situation in his new company cannot be worse than the one he is leaving. He must sometimes be warned that it may be; but there is no place for such warnings in the advertisement unless a nil response is required.

This leads to consideration of what is an optimum selection ratio, for this will determine the media chosen. Professor Northcote Parkinson once suggested that an ideal method of selection was to advertise in such forbidding terms that only one candidate – an ideal candidate – would apply. A selection consultant colleague, who was impressed by this idea, tried it out and received no replies. Another colleague advertised nationally for non-executive directors, quoting no excluding circumstances, and received 750 replies. Unfortunately, as only one client showed any interest in making such an appointment, he had the considerable task of disappointing 749 senior executives without causing offence.

Between these two extremes there is a happy medium to be struck. The danger of an inadequate response must be avoided, but the cost-effective objective is to have a small number of highly relevant candidates.

Choosing the Media

In the example quoted, the following considerations were taken into account when choosing the media.

1. Was the response required to be large and general, or small and specific? 'Small and specific' ruled out advertising on TV, radio or London Transport, and favoured *Accountancy Age*, whose readership consists mainly of accountants.

2. Would the candidates be in the immediate locality, in the region, in the country, or could they come from abroad? Accountants are notoriously difficult to move from one part of the country to another, as they are keenly aware of the costs and the problems of selling one house and buying another. South London housing is particularly expensive, so there will be no response from candidates who are unwilling to move to, or do not wish to live in, South London. So *The Financial Times* and *The Times*, whose readership is concentrated on London, may be justified to attract London-based candidates. On the other hand, this appointment is specific as to industry as well as to function, and if a candidate is willing to contemplate a move, distance is immaterial. So *The Sunday Times* is included both for its huge circulation but also for its considerable national and international coverage.

3. What is an acceptable timescale for replies? How immediate should the response be? The international response from *The Sunday Times* takes up to three weeks to arrive, so this was the timescale accepted. But the need for an early appointment biased the media selection in favour of daily papers and at the most, weekly papers. If a three-month timescale is tolerable, monthly or quarterly specialist journals can be very cost-effective. For example the monthly *Appointments Memorandum of the British Psychological Society* is only one seventh of the cost of *The Sunday Times*, but will produce a much better response for psychological appointments, and similar considerations apply for personnel managers and market researchers. So appointments in these fields advertised in the national press are few and far between.

On the other hand, if a large general response is immediately required, local radio or television may produce it. The economics of buying these media are stringent, as an advertisement at prime time costs several times as much as one in off-peak time, and they require a message which can be delivered in under twenty seconds, so that economy of words is crucial.

4. Does the age, salary or level of appointment pose special requirements? *The Accountant* or *The Observer* might have been chosen had the age limit been lower. Had the salary been lower, a tabloid newspaper might have been used.

	SUNDAY TIMES	FINANCIAL TIMES	THE TIMES	ACCOUNTANCY AGE	TOTAL
Display rate cost per single column centimetre	£56*	£34.50	£20	£33.88	£144.38
Cost of 26 s.c.c.	£1456	£897	£520	£880.88	£3753.88
Number of applicants	38	23	15	14	90
Cost per applicant	£38.32	£39	£34.7	£62.92	£42
Number interviewed	4	4	6	5	19
Cost per interview	£364	£224.25	£86.7	£176.18	£197.57
Number short-listed	1	1	1	1	4
Successful candidate from	—	—	1	—	1
Interviewing time (hours)	5	5	8	6	24
Cost @ £7 per hour	£35	£35	£56	£42	£168

Other media quoted by candidates				TOTAL	£3921.88

The Accountant
The Daily Telegraph   of which advertising cost is 96%.
The Observer.

* These costs are quoted as examples only, and cannot be used as a guide to current actual prices.

MEDIA COSTING SCHEDULE

Cost-Effectiveness of Media   In the example given, the decision has been taken to use four media: *The Sunday Times, The Financial Times, The Times* and *Accountancy Age*, and to have a display advertisement, thirteen cm. double column. Diagram II shows the result. Prospectively, or 'ex ante' as the economists would say, all four media seemed justifiable. 'Ex post', on reflection, some of the advertising money was wasted. Marketing managers are reputed to know that half of their advertising budget is wasted but they do not know which half. Personnel managers who collect this information do know which advertisements were worth while and which were wasted money; and however painful the knowledge may be at the time, it is valuable in ensuring that expensive mistakes are not repeated. In a positive sense, it allows media to be evaluated against each other, so that the most cost-effective can be used again; it also permits evaluation of the best timing, placing and content of advertisements. As these advertisements can cost, nowadays, far more than the cost of time involved in selection, monitoring them is an important aspect of cost-effective selection. An important point of detail is that the advertisement contains a different code letter for each medium, so that the source of the application can be accurately identified.

By the time that the ninetieth application has been received, the selector will be feeling that he has advertised too widely for one appointment, and that £3754 was too much to spend on advertising. By the time he has interviewed the nineteenth candidate he will be feeling that all the media have justified their inclusion in that they have all yielded a reasonable number of candidates worth interviewing, although the cheaper media are emerging as more cost-effective in terms of candidates worth interviewing. Retrospectively, or 'ex post', although each of the media justified themselves in producing one candidate for the short-list, only one candidate, from *The Times*, secured the post, so that all but £520 of the £3754 spent was in the end wasted. Having used all of these media effectively for one appointment or another the author did not wish to bias this hypothetical example too far in any particular direction. In practice, the more usual experience is that one or two of the media will produce all the candidates for the short-list. Learning from experience implies using only the most cost-effective media the next time.

The media themselves are enthusiastic in encouraging advertisers to place repeat advertisements; but in this field, repeat advertisements show sharply diminishing returns, and if additional money is available for advertising, it should be applied to increasing the number of media used. This procedure often provides access to a completely new readership, and allows discovery of highly cost-effective, but possibly low circulation media.

The Sunday Times can justify its high cost per single column centimetre by its extensive international readership. But if the requirement is only fifteen highly relevant candidates, over 99.9 per cent of its coverage is wasted. On the other hand, if the requirement is for a person who is one in 100,000 people, this degree of coverage may be necessary to secure him. This may lead to the reflection that for someone so exceptional, it may be cheaper to employ a headhunter to secure him by direct approach. But this is by no means the case: In contrast to America, where headhunting developed and where there is no national press, this country does have media with excellent national coverage, which are very effective in producing responses of high quality.

Timing and Positioning of Advertisements   There is a certain amount of folklore in advertising which claims that on a page of advertising, the top is better than the bottom position and the right-hand page better than the left. This is not supported by research. Sunday papers are so effective that Saturday, Monday and Tuesday suffer and are relatively ineffective. The midweek market becomes effective by Wednesday, and extends to Thursday and Friday. Far more important than any of these considerations are the effective title and compelling content, placed in the right medium.

The Economics of Data Capture

Once a field of candidates has been secured by advertising or other means, the economics of data capture come into operation. How these operate is probably best explained by a practical example in which the author was involved. The National Institute of Industrial Psychology received a call for help from the personnel manager of a firm in the steel industry in Sheffield. 'Our apprentice supervisor has taken ill and is in hospital,' he said. 'The whole works shuts down for its annual holiday in just over two weeks' time. Before then we have to have offers sent out to sixteen student apprentices and seventeen craft apprentices, chosen from 500 applications which we have received. We can provide you with a secretary full-time and I can spend about half my time on it. Can you help us meet the deadline?' The answer was 'yes' and the task was duly accomplished within the time set.

A number of constraints emerged as important. One was **threat avoidance**. Only one candidate in fifteen would eventually be selected, and with that wealth of choice there was no possible excuse for selecting a failure. Indeed it could be argued that with such a wealth of choice, to select a failure would be a grave injustice to someone who would have been a success, but who lost this chance to someone less able. As a matter of justice, **success seeking** was also important. Plainly, with this choice, many people who had the potential to do the job would be rejected, so as far as possible it was important that only those most likely to succeed would be selected.

Time was plainly very important. Assuming a forty-hour week, the time available for achieving the objective was 200 man-hours, which would be too easy to exceed. For example, giving every applicant a half hour interview would take 250 hours, so the selection became an exercise in efficient data capture. Enough information had to be secured from candidates to make them feel that they had been able to make their case as good candidates – particularly the better candidates. Enough information had to be secured to remove all doubts from the minds of the selectors as to whether they were selecting successes or failures; and the best assurance of this was to collect information known to be associated with success. Moreover, the methods of collecting the data had to take as little administrative time as possible; time was precious.

Fortunately, the company was one which had had an apprentice selection test battery installed by the National Institute of

Industrial Psychology a few years previously. In line with standard NIIP practice, the installation of the battery had been preceded by a comprehensive study of the job requirements of an apprentice, so that a job description detailing what would be expected of an apprentice, and a personnel specification describing what sort of person would be required was already on record. The installation also provided a comprehensive application blank and from the start it was possible to compare candidates on the basis of this completed application form. The consultant and the senior personnel manager each spent a full day studying the completed application blanks, weighing up which candidates best met the most important requirements of the personnel specification, on paper at least; but taking account of the fact that the apprenticeship scheme could accommodate people from widely different backgrounds. They worked independently and compared their results at the end of the day. As a result, the initial list of 500 was cut by eighty per cent to a hundred candidates who, both agreed, were worth considering further.

The hundred candidates were invited for group testing in groups of twenty. The secretary had been trained in administration and marking of the tests and so shared the marking with the consultant. In the interests of urgency, the forty candidates who were agreed upon by the consultant and the senior personnel manager as being the 'best on paper' were invited for the first two test sessions. It was not assumed that 'best on paper' meant that all would be selected since this would imply that no more information would be required to make the selection. If selection decisions are to be made on a basis of full information, then the proper time for final decisions to select is after all the information has been collected. With preliminary instructions, candidates took three hours to complete the battery. Time taken up to the point of testing was four senior management days and two secretary days. Group testing of one hundred candidates in five groups of twenty took two and a half days of consultant and secretary time, with one group being tested each morning and one group each afternoon, with marking proceeding while the tests were being administered.

From the test results fifty candidates were rejected, fifty selected for interview. Each candidate was given three interviews of ten minutes by three assessors in sequence: a member of the engineering staff, the senior personnel manager and the consultant. The first interviewer in these 'one-to-one' interviews

provided briefing notes for subsequent interviewers on:
- (a) areas not covered and gaps in the information;
- (b) points requiring further investigation;
- (c) points of special interest.

This took twenty-five hours of management time. The three interviewers subsequently met together for three hours to discuss all the information which took nine hours of management time. While the interviewing was taking place, the secretary completed standard letters of rejection to the 450 candidates and in the final stage sent thirty-three letters of offer and rejected the remaining candidates.

As a basis for costing in this example, we can take *The Financial Times* figure that the median salary in the middle of 1982 for a senior manager just below the level of director was £13,450 per annum. With a four-week holiday and a five-day week, this gives 240 working days in the year. Allowing for an eight hour day gives 1920 hours per annum, and a cost of £7 per hour. The cost of the secretary can be put at half this amount, say £3.50 per hour.

Reduction of 500 applicants to 100 invited for interview:
Personnel Manager: 16 hours; consultant: 16 hours;
secretary: 16 hours = 40 hours at £7 per hour =   £280.00

Group testing of 100 candidates and reduction to 50:
Consultant: 20 hours; secretary 20 hours
= 30 hours at £7 per hour =   £210.00

50 candidate interviews:
Consultant: 8.3 hours; engineer: 8.3 hours;
personnel manager: 8.3 hours
= 25 hours at £7 per hour =   £175.00

Final decision discussion: ı:	9 hours at £7 per hour =	£ 63.00
100 invitations for test = secretary: 10 hours	=	£ 35.00
33 offer letters = secretary: 11 hours	=	£ 38.50
467 rejection letters = secretary: 23 hours	=	£ 80.50

£882.00

There may be criticism that this is a somewhat artificial calculation as the consultant was bound to be paid for the entire eighty hours in the two weeks (cost £650), and that the secretary was involved for the entire eighty hours of the two weeks (cost £280). Much more important was that a satisfactory conclusion was reached within two weeks using only three and a half days of the personnel manager's time and one and a half days of the engineer's time.

This example of efficient data capture is worth analysing in three ways: in terms of the reliability and validity of the methods used; the function performed by each part of the selection process, and the economic importance of using the techniques in the right order.

Analysis of application forms

Of all techniques of selection, the application form is the most underrated by the inexperienced selector; this is because its demands are less immediate and its potential less obvious. An interview is obviously a real-time challenge, and interviewing a high-level skill. Even experienced interviewers exert effort to maintain their skills at a high level; but analysis and interpretation of application forms is a learning experience which can continue through life. Yet what an experienced selector can reliably deduce from an application form is not a subject on which the learned journals are very informative.

Galton (1902) first observed that a good predictor of what a man will do in the future is what he has done in the past, and Goldsmith (1922) gave one of the first accounts of the potential of the personal history blank in the selection of salesmen. But generally it was taken for granted as a traditional aid to the selector, while Guilford (1959), a psychometrician, commented 'biodata research has been characterised by an empirical shotgun approach largely devoid of both theory and generality.' Guilford was right since the interpretation of application forms is an empirical skill and situation-specific, because what is relevant in an application form depends crucially on the job for which the applicant is being considered, and achieving generality is therefore difficult. He may have been right in suggesting that the research reported to that point was largely devoid of theory and generality; but he was mistaken if he thought that the approach would be impossible to use over a wide variety of jobs because it lacked consistent principles of application and a sound basis in psychological theory. One of the real virtues of the **Seven Point Plan** (Rodger) is that it provides a systematic set of principles for the collection of biographical data.

Of recent years a much better appreciation of the application form or **personal history form** has developed under the heading of **biographical data research**, and with the application of computers to discovering associations, **biodata research** seems assured of a good future. Monahan and Muchinsky (1983) indicate that from the 1950s to the 1970s the percentage of studies using biodata as predictions in validity studies increased from eight per cent to twenty-eight per cent. Reilly and Chao (1982), in another review of validity studies, found that biodata provided the most valid predictions of reliability and job proficiency. They comment that 'biographical information or biodata has a long history of use in industry, but it was not until 1950 that biodata became widely used as part of selection systems.' The reliability and predictive power of biodata has been strongly supported by Owens (1966) in a comprehensive review of research and practice. He comments that 'the predictions of Galton have been amply fulfilled. Past behaviour as recorded in background data is indeed an excellent predictor of future behaviour.'

To return to our example, the reduction of 500 invited applications to one hundred candidates invited for test was a significant indicator of the reliance placed on this technique not to accept potential failures or reject potential successes. This was not a matter of forming general impressions by reading letters of application. Although they published little on the subject, the National Institute of Industrial Psychology taught consistent principles for the analysis of biographical data, based on the Seven Point Plan and a standard application form. Letters of application were distrusted as non-standard, inadequate and unreliable indicators of the ability of candidates. The comprehensiveness of the standard application form for engineering apprentices led to a high degree of agreement between the consultant and the personnel manager as to the one hundred candidates who would proceed to the next stage. As to the function performed by this technique, as well as providing a basis for choosing the better candidates, the application form gave rise to a number of hypotheses as to the personality of the individual, which required to be tested at interview.

In terms of the Seven Point Plan, the application form can provide a considerable amount of information on **Attainments, Interests,** and **Circumstances,** but on **Physique, Disposition, Intelligence** and **Special Aptitudes** only tentative inferences can be made, to be tested later. As to the economics of this technique, it is the most valuable of all techniques. Application forms can be completed by candidates at any time or place convenient to them. If they are keen on the job they will take pains to complete the form well; if they are less keen or have little of relevance to offer, they will not return it. The selectors in turn can study these at any suitable time and place; and provided the personnel specification is clear and accurate, experience in picking out the most relevant features is rapidly gained, and decisions can be made quite quickly. Over a longer period, the personnel manager can become quite an expert in what is to be expected from a given school, educational or technical qualification, or district, or family background, and all of this can be applied in the interpretation. In the economics of selection it is a reliable principle that it is more worth while for a selector to spend a further hour studying personal history forms and reducing the number to be interviewed, than to waste that hour interviewing someone who was not worth seeing.

Psychological Testing   Psychological testing as a method of data capture in selection is really the application to humans of scientific principles of observation and measurement: when a meteorologist wants to measure wind speed he ensures, in the interests of securing accurate, reliable and unbiased data, that the equipment is designed to do so accurately and reliably, and insists that certain rules are followed in its use and interpretation. If the measuring instrument is properly set up, and the rules are followed, it will produce a much more accurate result than a skilled observer could produce from watching trees or spindrift, or throwing grass in the air. In the same way, psychological tests are designed for accurate measurement. They need to be used according to standard rules, but provided this is done they produce results which are more objective and accurate than those of an interviewer. A companion booklet in this series, 'Testing in Selection Decisions' by G. M. Bolton (1983) considers tests in much more detail than is possible here. Our concern will be the economics of their use, the function which they perform in selection and their validity and reliability in use.

The test battery used in our practical example was described in NIIP Report No. 14 *Tests for Engineering Apprentices – A Validation Study* by Frisby, Vincent and Lancashire (1959). It consisted of Group Test 70 (non-verbal intelligence); Group Test 33 (verbal intelligence); Form Relations (spatial judgment); EA2

(Engineering Arithmetic); Vincent Mechanical Models (Mechanical Judgment); and Mechanical Information. The validity of the battery is embodied in the report. As to reliability, it is safe to say that the reliability of psychological tests is seldom a matter of doubt. Their reliability is usually higher than that of the criterion used to validate them.

As to the function which psychological tests performed, it has been mentioned that from application forms only tentative inferences can be made about General Intelligence and Special Aptitudes. Group Test 70 and Group Test 33 provided the necessary evidence for conclusions to be drawn about mental energy, reasoning capacity and general ability. The other tests provided information on the level of relevant special aptitudes. EA2 was particularly important: if teachers had failed to teach a 16 year-old how to add, subtract, multiply and divide with any competence, he would fail to be an engineer of any competence. Borderline candidates were those with good academic records who did badly on the tests; these could be pupils of limited ability, but educable and persevering. Rather better prospects were candidates with relatively poor academic records but high test results. Although basically able, they had decided that school had nothing more to offer them, but were anxious to prove themselves in a more practical working role. In economic terms, psychological testing is at its most efficient where large numbers of candidates can be brought together for group testing. It provides candidates with practical challenges, and the opportunity of showing what they can do, but is economical in administrative time, and marking of large numbers of tests although boring and requiring concentration can be very efficiently and quickly accomplished.

Group testing is most practicable where firms are engaging a large intake of candidates at the start of their careers seeking their first post. In such cases, candidates are likely to gain assurance from being with other candidates, rather than being upset by them. Within a company, too, some groups of people can be brought together for testing without problems.

However, in appointing a finance director, as in our advertising example, several candidates who might know each other might consider being tested in a group as an invasion of their privacy, and individual testing becomes necessary. Psychological testing then loses its economic advantages and reverts to the status of an extended objective interview. Two tests in the engineering apprentice selection battery were omitted in the example given as likely to take too much time. The Stenquist Test is a practical mechanical assembly test and the RV Manual is a test of hand steadiness and finger control. As performance, rather than paper and pencil tests, they required a set of equipment for each person tested; and the Stenquist in particular required the administrator, after scoring, to dismantle the objects assembled. Like performance tests, work sample tests often have the problem that they require a set of equipment for each candidate tested, and so must be given individually. However, given in conjunction with the interview, they may provide useful information not only about level of ability, but will distinguish between those who achieve their results by feverish if somewhat random activity and those who get there by being methodical, if rather more slowly.

Assessment of Disposition, the Seven Point Plan term for personality, was left to the interview stage of apprentice selection. At that age personality characteristics are less well formed, and measurement is likely to be less accurate and reliable. Some aspects of adult personality also change as part of an adaptation to new circumstances and challenges, but the underlying personality is more established and measurable, as well as being more important.

A comprehensive psychological test battery, including personality tests, may be used where the individual is being seen as part of a long-term investment in human capital, where an assessment has to be made as to how well the person will fit the organisation, and where there may be occupational assets which could be better utilised in transfer or promotion. In such cases the aim is to carry out a profiling operation with several widely differing tests, which will reveal a pattern of strengths and weaknesses. This approach is also of value in employing disabled people. There can be considerable advantages in employing disabled people, providing the profile of their abilities and disabilities is established. Disablement is a medical rather than an occupational category, and what a disabled person cannot do may not be significant for many jobs. Once employed, the disabled have a long-term economic pay-off, usually proving dependable as long-term employees – diligent workers who are seldom absent. Here, psychological testing can produce a profile of the positive abilities of the disabled person which can be translated into the jobs which they can do.

In general, psychological tests have much to recommend them as efficient methods of data capture, particularly where large intakes are concerned. Even with small numbers of employees an employer can, over a period of time, use them to determine minimum and maximum standards for any job, and can maintain these standards from year to year independent of the source of candidates or the place of testing, and irrespective of the assessor. All other standards are liable to change, not just from year to year, but often from before lunch to after it.

Interviewing   As a technique of selection, interviewing occupies a paradoxical position. On the one hand it is regarded as a completely necessary part of a selection procedure and may be the only technique employed. On the other hand, it has been rightly condemned as unreliable, inaccurate, subjective and uneconomic. Over fifty years ago in some of the earliest investigations, Scott (1915) and later Hollingsworth (1930) demonstrated how unreliable the interview could be. Other researchers have shown that because of its unreliability it is likely to reduce the validity of a selection procedure rather than increase it. In the practical example given, the interview was left until the last stage of the procedure, with only fifty of the 500 applicants remaining, but where each assessor would have in front of him a comprehensive application form and a complete set of test results for each candidate.

In terms of the Seven Point Plan there remained questions concerning Physique; did the candidate appear fit, with eyesight, hearing, speech and general physique adequate for an engineering apprentice? As to Disposition, what sort of person was he? Was he dominant or docile? Was he reliable? Had he any distastes which could make for unhappiness in the job? Finally, there were hypotheses formed from studying the application form, which could only be confirmed by direct questioning. Sequential interviews were used, and these took the weight of interviewing away from the engineer, who concentrated on physique, on identifying points of special interest in the candidate and on points about which he was doubtful. The personnel manager took the second interview, and concentrated on verifying hypotheses and dispositional topics, and the consultant investigated any unanswered questions. This was economical interviewing; had the team interviewed as a panel it would have taken three times as long. The ten-minute interview may seem very short, but it should be remembered that candidates were young, had no job history to explore and that the function of the interview had been restricted to securing information not available by other means. It should be noted also that the function of the interview was one of data capture and not of decision-making. The final decisions were taken at a discussion at which all the information was reviewed systematically before a decision was taken.

Handyside and Duncan (1953), in validating a selection scheme for supervisors, highlighted the problem of interviewing when they discovered that an untrained interviewer could have a reliability as low as +0.15 while that of a trained interviewer could be as high as +0.66. Eysenck (1955) has always been a trenchant critic of interviewing, basing his assertions on the researches of Scott and Hollingsworth. However, on investigating these earlier researches, those involved in training personnel executives and managers in selection discovered that they referred (a) to untrained interviewers (b) working without job descriptions or personnel specifications (c) who had no plan for the interview or for data capture.

In practice, the skill of an interviewer can be improved dramatically by even a short period of training backed up by monitored practice. To have a job description and a personnel specification is invaluable in focussing the interview, which should always be run as a plan for data capture.

Interviewing still remains the least efficient method of data capture, because it is specific to a time and place and because of the danger that decision-making in the early part of an interview will interfere with the process of data capture. As far as possible, data capture should come first, so that candidates are considered in the light of all the relevant information. Information processing of the data should be done systematically and objectively, and the decision-making should come after comprehensive consideration of all the candidates. Results of psychological research have suggested that managers are good decision-makers in the presence of inadequate information, but that their capacity for information processing leaves much to be desired. The danger in selection, as in many other activities, is that of too much decision-making too early, before all the relevant information has been collected.

Interviews as a data capture device make considerable demands on the interviewer. They demand continuous cognitive alertness and energetic recording activity combined with a relaxed emotional state. Untrained interviewers too readily become emotionally involved in the process, and become subject to the twin dangers of overrating poor candidates because they like them, and rejecting good candidates too soon.

A companion booklet in this series, *Interviewing for Selection Decisions* by G. M. Bolton (1983), gives a much more detailed account of the use and function of the interview than is possible here. Suffice it to say that most selection interviews are imperfect and that even good interviewers have to keep in practice. If cost-effectiveness is the aim because of the high skill level demanded, and because of the relatively low reliability of the technique, interviews should be avoided as far as possible. For most jobs, it will be necessary to have an interview at some stage, but poor interviewing may not produce any gain in reliable information compared with other sources.

Ordering of Techniques

Economics has been called the dismal science because most of its principles seem to suggest that ideals are not attainable, and that you can never have enough of what you want. However, the study of the economics of selection yields a brighter picture, because in data capture the techniques most economical of administrative time are also the most reliable and capable of providing the best predictors.

The principles worth following can be summarised as follows:
1. Time taken in preparing a thorough job description and a comprehensive specification is never wasted. It pays to know what you are looking for.
2. Particularly where large intakes are in prospect, or where there are many people doing the same job, it is worth conducting biodata research so that all information with a known significance for success in the job can be collected as early as possible.
3. Candidates who are interested in a job appreciate the opportunity of expanding on their relevant experience, which is provided by a comprehensive application form. Special supplements to a standard form can usefully be developed for jobs with special requirements, and thus maximise the use made of the application form.

4. Where many people are doing the same job, and turnover is significant, it is worth while having advertising campaigns with regular intakes. Recruitment by penny numbers is more costly.
5. Group testing should be used as far as possible. Larger intakes may make this more feasible.
6. Reserve interviewing and other techniques, which are expensive of administrative time, to the final stages of selection. Panel interviews in particular should be avoided as they are both unreliable and expensive.

The Economics of Validation

Up to now, this account has been concerned with cost-benefit aspects of selection and with making sure that selection avoids unnecessary waste of money, while meeting certain positive criteria of efficiency. There is still, however, the unpleasant prospect that the candidate who is efficiently selected at minimum cost may be unsatisfactory. Selection of a candidate is a prediction of success: but what sort of success? And for how long is the prediction good? What is the pay-off for spending time and money on complicated selection procedures, as against hiring anyone who turns up and firing them promptly if they are no use?

These are the questions which arise when considering the economics of validation, and as before they can be considered under the three headings: **threat avoidance, success seeking** and **candidate optimisation.**

Threat Avoidance

Threat avoidance needs to be attended to as soon as a decision has been made that the candidate is worth a job offer. Competition for jobs is such that candidates typically apply for several jobs and the best candidates may have several job offers to consider. It is therefore necessary to make a job offer quickly in writing. If the post is subject to references or security clearance, the starting date offered can be delayed but the offer should be made.

Bargaining by candidates by using one offer to improve the conditions of a second offer is exceptional, particularly amongst younger candidates, who are likely to accept the first offer made. The Civil Service suffers greatly from this, for although the selection procedures are valid and efficient, many good candidates are lost to them because the offer comes months rather than days after the selection boards. That another employer offered first is only one threat: other threats can arise from the circumstances of the applicant and the conditions of employment offered. Inability to sell a house, or finance a new one, or even finance the removal if removal expenses are inadequate, can all cause candidates to refuse offers. We have criticised the interview, but one of its essential functions is to verify that the terms and conditions of appointment are acceptable to the candidate, and to elucidate and face any logistic problems which might prevent the offer being accepted. In addition, care must be taken to leave with the candidate such a favourable impression of the company that the likelihood of an offer being accepted is maximised. Selection which results in offers being turned down fails at the first test for validity.

The threat does not disappear when the candidate joins the company. Statistical analysis of the influences making for survival in jobs has revealed that two countervailing forces are at work: a **force of alienation** which is strongest when employees join a new organisation, but which is dispelled in time: and a **force of attachment** which is weakest when employees join, but which gains in strength in time.

Candidates coming from previous employment normally assume that the 'bad news' – the irritations of work – cannot be worse than that with the employer they are leaving. The rude shock that this is not always so is worst in the first days of employment, when employer, colleagues, and subordinates may all seem alien and hostile, and working conditions most intolerable. Some of this may be overcome by systematic induction procedures and the difficulties of the job may be mitigated by systematic training. The forces of attachment can also be increased by these measures. But if the selection procedures have failed to detect that the candidate lacks the ability to meet training targets, or has the wrong personality for the post, then the distastes of doing the job, and the difficulties in learning the job may lead to an early departure. So the second test of the validity of a selection procedure is whether the candidate, having arrived for work, survives.

Threat avoidance in the longer term is a matter of risk limitation, the risks being in the form of **critical incidents.** Systematic selection can fairly easily guarantee that candidates recruited have the ability to produce a performance which is adequate to survive in a job. What is much more difficult is to assess a candidate's risk of failure through a critical incident. This may be an expensive mistake or even an unfortunate accident, but it is the precipitating event which may lead to a borderline performer, sometimes even a good performer, being asked to resign.

The type of critical incident most likely in the job is usually obvious from the job description, so in selection the process of risk assessment is one of judging its probability in the individual. If threat avoidance were the only option in selection, the emphasis would be heavily on stigma-hunting, discovering the weaknesses of candidates as a reason for rejecting them.

Success Seeking

Fortunately success seeking also has an important place. This is not only a matter of job description as suggested earlier; of defining the requirements of the job and its objectives, and translating this into terms of the sort of candidate required. There are also considerable possibilities for experiment, particularly where there are reasonable numbers of employees. This involves asking, 'who are the successful people in this job?' followed by, 'what makes them successful?' Where there are possibilities of using tests in selection, a useful preliminary may be to try out some which seem relevant to the job to be done, and see whether any of them have concurrent validity, that is, can distinguish the best from the not so good. One drawback of this is that failures are probably no longer employed, but even a modest positive correlation (say $+.25$) of the test with the success-failure criterion will make it worth using. Tests are usually more reliable than the criteria they predict.

Having one main criterion for success is gratifyingly simple, since the selection effort can then be devoted to identifying this one characteristic in the candidate. But however useful it may be to have only one criterion of success, it is important not to oversimplify the issue. Much more usually there may be several virtues making for success, and there may even be a conflict of criteria so that they are never all combined in the same individual. The vital consideration is then to have them rank ordered in terms of importance, so that the lack of one quality may be traded off against the presence of another.

Whatever the job, one criterion of success is likely to be the good opinion of the manager immediately senior, and apart from survival this is the second most important criterion in assessing the predictive capacity of a selection procedure. Even if the individual has left, the question 'was his leaving a matter of regret or relief?', can be an important one in determining whether selection is on the right lines. Once a candidate has been selected, success seeking has a very positive role to play, involving maximising the income earning potential of the candidate as soon as possible. This does not mean dispensing with induction and training, for such enthusiasm can be self-defeating, but it does mean remembering that the best candidates settle in and absorb training more quickly. So with a flexible training schedule a good candidate can be provided with early challenge and given an early opportunity to be a success. One of the surprises for the psychologist in selection is that some of the most prejudiced and least objective of employers can pick successes, because they provide so much encouragement and place such faith in their candidates that they literally make successes out of them.

Candidate Optimisation

Because there may be several criteria of success and because a wide variety of candidates have the possibility of success the personnel specification is necessarily an ideal picture. On being reviewed, it may produce the distinct impression that it is unlikely that such a paragon exists, and it is usually too discouraging to show to candidates. However, the essence of the exercise is to have high standards and to attempt to achieve them, remembering that although one may set out to look for a five legged man, one has eventually to settle for one with two or even one.

Candidate optimisation in selection is ensuring that the candidate with the strongest two legs is selected. Once a candidate has been selected, candidate optimisation takes full account of the strengths and weaknesses of the candidate particularly in relation to the stated criteria. Some weaknesses, such as the wrong style of hair or dress, poor telephone manner or lack of customer awareness can be quickly overcome. Deficiencies in knowledge and experience can be remedied by training; but disabilities compared with the ideal may remain. These are characteristics of the individual which cannot be remedied by training and have to be accepted as basic to the individual and his or her style. An optimising manpower policy will provide scope for balancing such disabilities with strengths in another direction, deploying the individual in such a way that failure is avoided.

A static view of validation is to wait until people prove to be failures so that they can be added to the count of failures. A proactive view is to perceive areas in which people need support, quite possibly to avoid critical incidents and help them to turn potential failure into success. A chairman of a company, for instance, can do this for himself by employing an expert in public relations, if he has weaknesses in writing or making public statements. It is less usual to identify that support is needed for a professional engineer who is weak in grammar and yet has to write to clients. Validation of selection procedures can be used to identify the causes of problems after selection and training, feeding back the diagnosis to those responsible for selecting, training and supervising the employees. In this way, we can help to ensure that our investment at the selection stage is as fully economic as possible.

Appendix

Checklist for Advertisements

Does it **inform** the candidates:
(1) what kind of company the successful applicant will be working for?
(2) where he or she will work?
(3) what his or her title will be?
(4) to whom he or she will be responsible?
(5) what functions or persons he or she will be responsible for?
(6) what the ideal candidate's age, qualifications and experience must be?

Does it **attract** attention?
(1) Is the advertisement in the right medium to attract the kind of person you are looking for?
(2) Have you used enough separate media?
(3) Is the job title clear enough and large enough to attract attention?
(4) Is the advertisement a contribution to the public image of the company?
(5) Has the company something to be proud of which could be mentioned in the advertisement?
(6) Have you managed to make it just a little different from the rest?

Does it stimulate **desire** by mentioning the rewards?
(1) What is the minimum salary?
(2) What other rewards go with the job?
(3) What other advantages are there in working for the company?

Does it have instructions for **action**: where to write; with what; for what; by when; to whom?

And also: could you cut out some of the unnecessary words? Have you sufficiently narrowed the field?

References

BECKER, G. S. (1964). *Human Capital*. New York: Columbia University Press. (p. 8)

BOLTON, G. M. (1983). *Interviewing for Selection Decisions*. Windsor: NFER-NELSON. (p. 29)

BOLTON, G. M. (1983). *Testing in Selection Decisions*. Windsor: NFER-NELSON. (p. 24)

BRIDGE, J. (1981). *Economics in Personnel Management*. London: IPM. (p. 8)

BRUMMET, R. L., PYLE, W. C., and FLAMHOLTZ, R. G. (1969). 'Human resource measurement – a challenge for accountants', *Personnel Administration*: July. (p. 8)

CANNON, J. (1979). *Cost Effective Personnel Decisions*. London: IPM. (p. 8)

CYERT, R. M., and MARCH, J. G. (1963). *A Behavioural Theory of the Firm*. Englewood Cliffs, New Jersey: Prentice Hall. (p. 8)

EYSENCK, H. J. (1953). *Uses and Abuses of Psychology*. Harmondsworth: Penguin Books. (p. 28)

FISHER, I. (1906). *The Nature of Capital and Income*. London: Macmillan. (p. 4)

FRISBY, C. B., VINCENT, D. F., and LANCASHIRE, R. (1959). *Tests for Engineering Apprentices: A Validation Study*. NIIP Report No. 14. (p. 24)

GALTON, F. (1902). *Life History Album*. New York: Macmillan. (p. 22)

GILES, W. J., and ROBINSON, D. F. (1972). *Human Resource Accounting*. London: IPM. (p. 8)

GOLDSMITH, D. B. (1922). 'The use of the personal history blank as a salesmanship test', *Journal of Applied Psychology*, vol. 28, no. 1, 149–55. (p. 22)

GUILFORD, J. P. (1959). *Personality*. New York: McGraw-Hill. (p. 22)

HANDYSIDE, J. D., and DUNCAN, D. C. (1954). *Occupational Psychology*, vol. 28, no. 1, 19–23. (p. 28)

HERZBERG, F. (1966). *Work and the Nature of Man*. New York: World. (p. 14)

HOLLINGSWORTH, H. L. (1930). *Vocational Psychology and Character Analysis*. New York: Appleton. (pp. 27, 28)

LIKERT, R. (1967). *The Human Organisation, its Management and Value*. New York: McGraw-Hill. (p. 8)

MONAHAN, C. J. and MUCHINSKY, P. M. (1983). 'Three decades of personnel selection research', *Journal of Occupational Psychology*, vol. 56, 215–25. (pp. 4, 23)

OWENS, W. A. (1976). 'Background Data'. Chapter 14 in DUNNETTE, M.D. (Ed) Handbook of *Industrial and Organisational Psychology*. Chicago: Rand McNally. (p. 23)

RODGER, A. (1974). *The Seven Point Plan*. Windsor: NFER-NELSON. (NIIP Paper I Reprint) (p. 22)

REILLY, R. R. and CHAO, G.T. (1982). 'Validity and fairness of some alternative employee selection procedures. *Personnel Psychology*. vol. 35, 1–62. (p. 23)

ROBBINS, L. (1932). *The Nature and Significance of Economic Science*. London: Macmillan. (p. 3)

SCHULTZ, T. W. (1961). 'Investment in human capital', *American Economic Review*, March. (p. 8)

SCOTT, W. D. (1915). 'The scientific selection of salesmen', *Advertising and Selling*, vol. 25, 5–6, 94–6. (pp. 27, 28)

SIMON, H. A. (1957). *Administrative Behaviour*. New York: Macmillan. (p. 8)

WILLIAMSON, O. E. (1963). 'Managerial discretion and business behaviour', *American Economic Review 1963*, pp. 32–57. (p. 8)

Bibliography

In addition to the references, the following will repay further study.

BRAMHAM, J., and COX, D. (1984). *Personnel Records and Computerisation*. London: IPM.

BRECH, E. F. L. (1965). *Organisation*. London: Longmans.

COURTIS, J. (1976). *Cost Effective Recruitment*. London: IPM.

DUNNETTE, M. D. (Ed) (1983). Handbook of *Industrial and Organisational Psychology*. Chichester: Wiley.

GUEST, D., and KENNY, T. (Eds) (1983). *A Textbook of Techniques and Strategies in Personnel Management*. London: IPM.

HOLDSWORTH, R. F. (1972). *Personnel Selection Testing*. London: BIM.

KENNEY, J., DONNELLY, E., and REID, M. (1979). *Manpower Training and Development*. London: IPM.

MACKENZIE DAVEY, D., and McDONNELL, P. (1983). *How to Interview*. London: BIM.

PLUMBLEY, P. (1976). *Recruitment and Selection*. London: IPM.

PUGH, D. S., and HICKSON, C. R. (1971). *Writers on Organisations*. Harmondsworth: Penguin.

RAY, M. E. (1980). *Recruitment Advertising*. London: Business Books.

REVANS, R. W. (1971). *Developing Effective Managers*. London: Longmans.

RIBEAUX, P., and POPPLETON, S. E. (1978). *Psychology and Work*. London: Macmillan.

SEYMOUR, W. D. (1968). *Skills Analysis Training*. London: Pitman.

STEWART, A., and STEWART, V. (1978). *Tomorrow's Men Today*. London: IPM.

TALBOT, J. R., and ELLIS, C. D. (1969). *Analysis and Costing of Company Training*. London: Gower Press.

THOMASON, G. F. (1981). *A Textbook of Personnel Management*. London: IPM.

TIFFIN, J. and McCORMICK, E. J. (1969). *Industrial Psychology*. London: Allen & Unwin.

UNGERSON, B. (Ed) (1973). *Recruitment Handbook*. London: Gower Press.

UNGERSON, B. (1983). *How to write a Job Description*. London: IPM.

VITELES, M. S. (1962). *Industrial Psychology*. London: Jonathan Cape.

WARREN, A., and DOWNS, S. (1978). *Trainability Tests – A Practitioner's Guide*. Cambridge: ITRU.

YOUNGMAN, M. *et al*. (1978). *Analysing Jobs*. Farnborough: Gower Press.

Index